ITALIA '90

SCOTLAND

Five In a Row

* * * * *

The Road to Rome

Dixon Blackstock
Sunday Mail

SPORTSPRINT PUBLISHING
EDINBURGH

Contents

© **John Donald Publishers Ltd., 1990**

John Donald Publishers Ltd.,
138 St. Stephen Street, Edinburgh EH3 5AA.

ISBN 0 85976 298 X

Our grateful thanks to the *Sunday Mail* and the *Scotsman and Evening News* for provision of the pictures used in this book. Also to Bob Thomas, Sports Photography, Northampton.

Phototypeset by Beecee Typesetting Services
Printed and bound in Great Britain by Billings & Sons Ltd., Worcester

Italy-ho

SCOTLAND WILL PLAY their Group C games in the port city of Genoa and the industrial centre at Turin.

The opening game against Costa Rica is at the 37,325 capacity Luigi Ferrari's stadium in Genoa, which was originally built in 1928 but has been totally reconstructed for the World Cup.

In fact, after a first attempt at alterations one side of the pitch was below the sight of the main stand . . . and the locals immediately dubbed it 'Stadium of the blind'. A hasty re-think had the pitch raised by three feet . . . which brings to mind the famous quote by film-maker Lord Grade about the soaring costs of the movie 'Raise the Titanic'. 'We would be cheaper lowering the Atlantic,' he observed.

The Scotland fans present for the opening fixture, which kicks off at 5.0 (which is 4.0 our time) on Monday June 11 will have no problems seeing the goals go in. Hopefully in the right net.

Next comes Sweden at the same venue on Saturday June 16, with a 9.0 start (8.0 in Scotland).

Temperatures in Genoa, which has a population of 726,000, will be in the 80s in June.

Scotland's final group game is against Brazil on Wednesday June 20 at Turin's new 67,411 stadium, Nuovo Communale, which has been built for the World Cup.

Turin is where the giant Fiat car company is based, and also houses the two famous club sides Torino and Juventus.

It is just under 100 miles from Genoa by road (take the A 21 or A 26) and there is a train service between the cities. Turin will also be in the 80s, but with a much higher humidity percentage.

Scotland: Five in a Row

The full list of World Cup groups and games is:

GROUP A

ITALY
AUSTRIA
USA
CZECHOSLOVAKIA

Saturday, June 9
Italy v Austria (Rome, 8.0)

Sunday, June 10
USA v Czechoslovakia
(Florence, 4.0)

Thursday, June 14
Italy v USA (Rome, 8.0)

Friday, June 15
Austria v Czechoslovakia
(Florence, 4.0)

Tuesday, June 19
Italy v Czechoslovakia
(Rome, 8.0)
Austria v USA (Florence, 8.0)

GROUP B

ARGENTINA
CAMEROON
USSR
RUMANIA

Friday, June 8
Arg v Cameroon (Milan, 5.0)

Saturday, June 9
USSR v Rumania
(Bari, 4.0)

Wednesday, June 13
Arg v USSR (Naples, 8.0)

Thursday, June 14
Cameroon v Rumania
(Bari, 8.0)

Monday, June 18
Argentina v Rumania
(Naples, 8.0)
Cameroon v USSR (Bari, 8.0)

GROUP C

BRAZIL
SWEDEN
COSTA RICA
SCOTLAND

Sunday, June 10
Brazil v Sweden
(Turin, 8.0)

Saturday, June 16
Brazil v Costa Rica
(Turin, 4.0)
Sweden v Scotland
(Genoa, 8.0)

Monday, June 11
Costa Rica v Scotland
(Genoa, 4.0)

Wednesday, June 20
Brazil v Scotland
(Turin, 8.0)
Sweden v Costa Rica
(Genoa, 8.0)

4

GROUP D

**WEST GERMANY
YUGOSLAVIA
UNITED ARAB EMIRATES
COLOMBIA**

Saturday, June 9
UAE v Colombia
(Bologna, 8.0)

Sunday, June 10
West Germany v Yugoslavia
(Milan, 8.0)

Thursday, June 14
Yugoslavia v Colombia
(Bologna, 4.0)

Friday, June 15
West Germany v UAE
(Milan, 8.0)

Tuesday, June 19
West Germany v Colombia
(Milan, 4.0)
Yugo v UAE (Bologna, 4.0)

GROUP E

**BELGIUM
SOUTH KOREA
URUGUAY
SPAIN**

Tuesday, June 12
Belgium v South Korea
(Verona, 4.0)

Wednesday, June 13
Uruguay v Spain
(Udine, 4.0)

Sunday, June 17
Belgium v Uruguay
(Verona, 8.0)
South Korea v Spain
(Udine, 8.0)

Thursday, June 21
Belgium v Spain
(Verona, 4.0)
South Korea v Uruguay
(Udine, 4.0)

GROUP F

**ENGLAND
REPUBLIC OF IRELAND
HOLLAND
EGYPT**

Monday, June 11
England v Rep of Ireland
(Cagliari, 8.0)

Saturday, June 16
England v Holland
(Cagliari, 8.0)

Tuesday, June 12
Holland v Egypt
(Palermo, 8.0)

Sunday, June 17
Rep of Ireland v Egypt
(Palermo, 4.0)

Thursday, June 21
England v Egypt (Cagliari, 8.0)
Republic of Ireland v Holland (Palermo, 8.0)

5

ITALIA '90

MILAN

UDINE

VERONA

TURIN

BOLOGNA

GENOA

FLORENCE

ROME

BARI

NAPLES

CAGLIARI

PALERMO

SCOTLAND
GROUP C

Brazil v Sweden
Turin : June 10

Costa Rica v **Scotland**
Genoa : June 11

Brazil v Costa Rica
Turin : June 16

Sweden v **Scotland**
Genoa : June 16

Brazil v **Scotland**
Turin : June 20

Sweden v Costa Rica
Genoa : June 20

The Road to Rome . . .

S COTLAND MAY NEVER HAVE a better chance of getting through to the second stages of the World Cup. For only EIGHT of the 24 teams in the finals will be eliminated after the first series of games. The top two teams in each of the six sections will go through: along with the four best third-placed sides.

There was a similar situation in Mexico last time . . . but the last hope vanished when Scotland failed to beat Uruguay in the final section game. The disappointing goalless draw, against a side which played almost the entire 90 minutes with 10 men, after a first-minute ordering off, meant the Scots failed to get third spot, and Uruguay went through instead with West Germany and Denmark.

'We know we have a great chance of making up for that in Italy,' says Dundee United's Maurice Malpas. 'Of course, it won't be easy. But the opportunity is there. This time we aim to take it.'

If they do, then the Scottish supporters are in for a rerr terr trying to sort out where they're heading for next. The trail could lead anywhere.

For instance, if Scotland WIN Group C, then they would play one of the third-placed sides from Group A, B or F in Turin on the afternoon of Sunday, June 24.

It's a lot simpler should the Scots finish RUNNERS-UP in the section: they would then meet the second-placed side from Group A, which features Italy, Austria, Czechoslovakia and USA. This game is scheduled for Bari, deep in the south of Italy, for the evening of Saturday, June 23.

7

Scotland . . . Five in a Row

The final option is finishing in THIRD, and this is where it gets really tricky. Where the Scots would end up for the next game is something that won't be decided until the last of the first-stage matches are over. You'll need your Italian road map at the ready for this one.

You could be in Naples on Saturday, June 23 for an afternoon kick-off against the winners of Group B, which has Argentina, Cameroon, Russia and Romania.

Alternatively, it might be Rome on Monday, June 25 for a meeting with the winners of Group A.

So there it is: Turin, Bari, Naples or Rome. Never mind the Tour de France, this is the Tour d'Italia.

The venues for the four quarter-final ties are Rome (June 30, evening): Florence (June 30, afternoon); Naples (July 1, evening) and Milan (July 1, afternoon).

The semi-finals are scheduled for July 3 in Naples and July 4 in Turin, both evening kick-offs.

Third place play-off will be in Bari on the evening of July 7 with the Grande Finale in Rome on the evening of Sunday, July 8.

Here We Go Again!

IT TOOK A BRAZILIAN JOURNALIST to sum up the Scottish disease.

'The trouble with the Scots is that although they admit England may have invented football, they believe is was Scotland who perfected the game,' he commented sourly after surveying the celebrations that went on after Scotland were drawn in the same section as Brazil for this year's World Cup Finals in Italy.

He's about half a century out in his verdict. Humiliations like Argentina in 1978 have knocked much of the swagger out of Scotland.

There always remains a certain amount of 'guid conceit'. But since we Scots invariably seem to top the League when it comes to heart trouble, cancer of every possible organ, alcoholism (and even recently gum disease!), why shouldn't we lead the way in harmless self-delusion as well?

There will be a few kilt-lifters among the thousands following Scotland to Italy this summer who actually believe their team will win the World Cup.

The majority will just be glad to be there, happy in the knowledge that it is better to have travelled hopefully than not to have travelled at all.

There is nothing in Scotland's World Cup record since they first entered the fray back in 1950 to encourage anything other than enjoyment of the experience while it lasts.

Brazil progress to the Finals with all the colour and flashing excitement of the samba; Italy get there in a slow, sleekit, smouldering tango; the Germans, naturally, simply trample over everyone in a ruthless march.

Scotland: Five in a Row

Scotland? Well, it's a bit like the old-fashioned square tango: two steps forward, one to the side, one back, one to the side and then off you go again.

Which naturally means exhilaration, frustration and depression. But that's Scotland for you.

There has not been a World Cup campaign yet that didn't feature bad results, squabbles on and off the field, money wrangles.

But don't think for a moment Scotland are unique in this. There is scarcely a country in the World that hasn't had similar kinds of trouble. It's just that we're too busy studying our own, and we fail to notice the others.

Scotland have come a long way since they made history in the 1950 competition by becoming the only country ever to knock itself out of the competition.

The S.F.A. in their lack of wisdom decreed that Scotland would only go to Brazil as holders of the Home International championship. They rebuffed an offer from F.I.F.A. offering a place if they finished runners-up . . . an arrangement England were quite happy to accept.

Up to the last minute before the deciding game between Scotland and England at Hampden, pleas were made to the S.F.A. to think again. They refused. England won the game and the title and travelled.

Scotland stayed at home and sulked.

Nowadays, the S.F.A. spend thousands of pounds in the long, involved preparations that are required to make it to the Finals . . . knowing full well the huge financial and psychological benefits which come in return.

The S.F.A. coffers will bulge with another £2 million in 1990. But it is not a matter of mere money. 'Everyone in Scotland walks a bit taller when we qualify,' declares recently retired S.F.A. secretary Ernie Walker.

He's right. Even non-football fans take a pride in Scotland's feat of qualifying for all five Finals since 1974.

Here We Go Again!

I know Rugby types like to point to New Zealand as an example of a small country which dominates in that particular sport. But that is a freak situation, and the number of countries competing at the highest level in rugby is limited.

Scotland, with a five million population, continually take on nations with a ten-fold advantage. Not unnaturally we often fail.

But amazingly we sometimes succeed. Every time we've made it to the Finals, great football nations have been left at home.

What wouldn't France, East Germany, Poland, Denmark, Bulgaria and our near neighbours Wales and Northern Ireland give to be putting themselves to the test against Brazil in Turin on June 20?

Five in a row: that's cause for celebration all right.

The Debacles

WE SHOULD HAVE KNOWN BETTER. History has prepared the Scottish fans to accept that the team only ever prefers to take the hard road.

'Everyone was too optimistic' is how captain Roy Aitken sums it up.

Maybe that Brazilian journalist is right, and the Scottish disease only needs to be fired by a wee bit success to bubble to the surface again. Sorry, senhor.

The reason for the optimism in September 1989 lay in the fact that after five section matches Scotland was sitting at the top of Group 5, with 9 out of 10 points.

And when Norway and France drew 1-1 in Oslo the night before the Scots were to face Yugoslavia in Zagreb, that left Scotland needing just one point from the last three games.

It was all over bar the singing. But the song was stillborn . . . dying in the dried-up throats of the fans who were to watch their team invent yet more new ways to prolong the agony.

IN YUGOSLAVIA it was two own goals.

IN FRANCE it was a collapse against 10 men. *Plus ça change,* as they are wont to say on the terracings at Firhill.

Andy Roxburgh had spelled it out all along that the Slavs were by far the strongest team in the group.

'We knew the hard bit was coming: the games against Yugoslavia and France away from home,' says Roy Aitken.

What he didn't know was just how hard. Or even how hard Scotland made it for themselves.

Ach well, any team that needed the hand of Joe (in the days before God decided to give Maradona a bit of help) to get through against Wales in 1977; or a Davie Cooper penalty against the same team five years later, was well used to a bit of drama.

Qualifying has even taken Scotland to the football outpost of Australia for a play-off.

So it really should have been no surprise that there were a couple of pieces of tough meat tucked away between the two slices of Norwegian smorgasbord.

And yet . . . there was a wee quiet air of confidence about the Scots as they set about their business in Zagreb on September 6, 1989.

Manager Roxburgh surprised the Slavs by slipping Gordon Durie into the fray. He was an unknown quantity. But not for long.

Scotland set out to 'take the sting out of the game.' They succeeded, to the extent that by half-time the 40,000 crowd at the Maksimir Stadium had fallen silent. Well, 39,000 had. The odd 1,000 were Scots who celebrated as first of all Ally McCoist put the ball in the net, only to have it disallowed.

Then, after 36 minutes, McCoist made space on the left to cross beautifully to the back post for Durie to score. The same partnership almost did it again just before half-time, but keeper Ivkovic came out quickly to save.

The Scots sang. The Slavs sulked. Then it was a case of enter the Dragan. Yugoslavia's brilliant midfield man Dragan Stojkovic, who had already shivered the timber in the first half, exploded on the scene after the break.

And at the same time Scotland, unbeknownst to the punters, had entered into a suicide pact.

Goalkeeper Jim Leighton came out to make a late, fatal leap at a Stojkovic cross. Missed. Katanec didn't.

That was in 54 minutes. And within minutes it was all over, with the talented Slavs getting the kind of helping head and foot they didn't need.

'We cut our own throats,' lamented boss Roxburgh as first of all Steve Nicol nodded a Stojkovic cross past

Scotland: Five in a Row

Leighton then a minute later team-mate Gary Gillespie was caught flat-footed by a cross and poked his attempted clearance into the net. Not the kind of double Liverpool usually produce.

A disconsolate Roxburgh reflected after the game: 'We prepared for two years for this one. The same mistakes won't be made against France . . . if nobody shoots us in the foot.'

A month later, Scotland contrived to deliver a bullet into each extremity.

The *entente* was stretched beyond cordiality at the Parc des Princes on October 11. For a start, the French did not extend the hand of friendship . . . it was *Le But* which was much in evidence.

McCoist, Johnston and Strachan were all chopped in a manner which would have set the needles clicking with approval in revolutionary days.

Two powerful headers from Richard Gough raised the morale of the 10,000 Scots on the terracings. Unfortunately it was the same Gough, who already had one hole in his foot after an operation which had laid him up for weeks, who first wounded Scotland.

The Ibrox man unaccountably misdirected a pass under no pressure. France reacted swiftly, the ball was shifted forward quickly and Deschamps squeezed a low shot into the net past Leighton at his post.

'Unforgivable,' said Roxburgh later about the goal. Whether he meant Gough or Leighton doesn't matter, since the Scotland boss is of a forgiving nature and anyway both are key players.

The damage was still reparable, and when the violent Di Meco was ordered off in the 57th minute for one foul too many, there was clearly still a chance for the Scots to put on a show.

The Debacles

They did. For one night only *Les Follies* transferred from Montmartre to the Parc des Princes.

The Scots high-kicked it forward in a flashing chorus line. And left the back of the stage empty for Cantona to clatter clear on a long ball and stick No. 2 past Leighton.

That was bad enough. It then became *très embarrassing* in the final minute when a shot from Durand deflected off Nicol and left Leighton doing the splits trying in vain to change direction.

Le débâcle was complete.

So it was on to Hampden, and the test against Norway. But not before those unpredictable Scots fans stood their ground like the students of the Bastille and demanded an appearance from the vanquished team.

It was the best move Scotland made all night when the losers came out to salute the real winners.

Song of Norway

IN THE BEGINNING there was Oslo. Bright, cheerful, friendly, expensive Oslo. Home of probably the dearest pint in the world.

Only a millionaire could be a lager lout in Norway.

The Tartan Army introduced community drinking. At £3 a pint they found this hard to swallow . . . so three of them would divvy up for the bevvy and take turns at sipping out the ONE pint!

When the draw was made in Zurich back on December 12, 1987 Scotland landed up in a five-team section with France, Yugoslavia, Norway and Cyprus.

S.F.A. secretary Ernie Walker, who immediately announced a programme of warm-up matches, said prophetically: 'It would be ideal for us to open with an away game against Norway next September, then play France at Hampden in October.'

He got half a wish. When the group five countries met in the shadow of the Eiffel Tower on February 9, 1988, four hours of tough talking brought Ernie his Oslo trip as planned.

But it was to be Yugoslavia for Hampden in October, and with the wily French using home advantage to the limit by fixing their final game in Paris against the weakest team, Cyprus . . . three days after all the other section games were finished.

Coach Henri Michel was clearly hoping that if by any chance France needed to score a barrowload to qualify, then it was on.

Only it wasn't. And he was off. He was deposed and

Roy Aitken congratulates Paul McStay after scoring against
Norway in Oslo.

replaced by national hero Michel Platini after a shock dropped point in October 1988 . . . against Les Misérables from Cyprus.

After the French said 'sacre bleu', they also said 'sack ra manager'.

By the time Scotland reached Oslo on September 14, 1988 they had played five build-up games. The only thing they had warmed up was the arguments.

Not even the helpful fact that there would be two qualifying places in a five-team section brought much solace after away draws against second-rate opposition like Saudi Arabia and Malta.

Goalless draws against Spain (away) and Colombia at Hampden were followed by a defeat from the Old Enemy at Wembley.

Words like 'shame' and 'embarrassing' were bandied around in the sports pages and provoked the normally moderate Roxburgh into a counter-attack: 'The criticism is quite excessive. I am really soured by the media attitude.'

Happily by the time the song of Norway was needed in September, everyone was in harmony again.

The Oslo encounter was Roxburgh's 17th in charge of Scotland, but of course his first World Cup tie. The articulate, meticulous former schoolteacher is one of the most sought-after and respected coaches in the world, as the constant demand for his presence at seminars under-lines.

His first task when he took over in 1986 was to build a sound international organisation. There would be no surprises like Chile or Iran. Detailed dossiers, many on video, are compiled on opponents and thousands of miles covered to get the details right.

He was also willing to give everyone a chance as he searched for the blend on the field as well . . . by the time he reached Oslo no fewer than 47 players had been involved in Scotland squads.

The winning goal at Oslo by Mo Johnston.

In his 16 games, Scotland had won four times, drawn eight and lost four. Only 11 goals had been conceded: but only 12 scored.

With Ally McCoist out injured, the Scotland boss after the customary warnings about the Norwegians being 'no mugs' went for a team to hold and command in midfield.

Skipper Roy Aitken had Paul McStay and Liverpool's Steve Nicol alongside him in the engine room while Mo Johnston, Brian McClair and young Kevin Gallacher were to carry the load up front . . . 'where you know you're going to get whacked,' quipped Gallacher.

As it turned out, the first whack was dispensed by Nicol

Scotland: Five in a Row

on the unfortunate Sundby who retired after just a few minutes to be replaced by Berg, who immediately learned the hard facts of life as viewed by Roy Aitken — a lesson neither the Norwegian nor the Italian referee Agnolin appreciated, and brought a booking for the Scottish captain.

By that time Scotland were ahead, with midfield man Paul McStay coming steaming into the box to thrash a loose ball home in the 14th minute.

Fjortoft equalised just before the break, however, to leave the Scots in a distinctly dodgy position. The Scots claimed for offside, but the referee was having none of it.

He wasn't for having much more of Aitken's abrasive approach and the Scots bench decided on a discreet retiral for Roy, pushing young Ian Durrant of Rangers into the battle, a move which helped send the flow of the game Scotland's way in the closing stages.

Finally it was Mo Johnston who was to give the Scots the dream start in the Ulleval Stadium where they hold the dream mile. He showed the striker's instinctive reaction in the 62nd minute when a blocked shot dropped awkwardly at his feet.

Off-balance or not, Mo slammed it home. It was a goal that not only set the ball rolling for Italy, it started the blond striker on his way to a wee bit of World Cup history as he plundered the net all the way through the campaign until he reached a record tally.

But even in victory there was controversy . . . naturally. So what's new?

The first rumblings were heard about the qualities, or supposed lack of them, of Roy Aitken as captain and midfield man. He was strongly defended by his boss, who did however admit that 'when he clattered one of their players in the second half and the referee walked away from it, I wasn't going to take the chance he would walk away the next time.'

Song of Norway

Scotland might have done away with the universally unpopular (apart from sales!) strip with the 'suspender belt' shorts. They hadn't dispensed with keeping their supporters in suspense.

Nevertheless, the mini tartan army celebrated . . . well, as best they could at Oslo prices. Andy Roxburgh even offered one fan a pound to help him enjoy himself — and was reminded this would scarcely buy a bag of crisps.

Just wait till you get to Italy, lads. Anything in a packet will cost a packet.

The Great Escape

IF STEVE McQUEEN had roared across the scene on a motor bike on the afternoon on February 8, 1989 it would not have been inappropriate.

For the lumpy, bumpy pitch at the Tsirion Stadium in Limassol, Cyprus was to be the setting for Scottish football's version of *The Great Escape*.

But in a new twist even Hollywood never dreamed of, it was a German who organised the escape route for the Scots.

Siegfried Kirschen didn't blow a hole in a wall to set the Scots free. He just didn't blow at all.

Because of blatant, and well publicised, time-wasting tactics by Cyprus, the East German referee allowed play to run . . . and run . . . and run.

When big Rangers defender Richard Gough, who had already secured at least a point for the Scots with an earlier equaliser, stationed himself at the back post for a free kick from the left by skipper Roy Aitken, the game had already gone an incredible five and a half minutes into overtime.

And the sight of Gough rising majestically to bullet in a header that meant victory had the thousands of Scots in attendance dancing in disbelief.

They were joined on the trackside by manager Roxburgh, who still winces with embarrassment at the TV evidence which proves conclusively that under the blazer and badge beats the heart of a fan.

The Cypriots were dancing too. A war dance. The friendly folk who had charmed the Scottish supporters forgot the fact that their island was supposed to be the home of Aphrodite, the Goddess of Love, and went looking for the referee.

A tense moment in Cyprus. Maurice Malpas clears the danger.

Luckily they didn't find him, but the riot scenes which accompanied their search were in time duly punished by F.I.F.A.

Andy Roxburgh, once he and his squad were safely en route home, revealed that the F.I.F.A. observer Dr George Szepesi had been made aware of the Cypriot penchant for play-acting at injuries and wasting time at goal kicks and throw-ins.

Word had obviously filtered down to referee Kirschen as well. But by general admission he was a brave man to let the game overrun by more than six minutes.

Scotland: Five in a Row

Another general admission was the Scots had, in the manager's words: 'Got out of jail.'

All his pre-match warnings about the pitch, the time-wasting, the injury tactics and especially the pious 'we have no chance' approach from the home side, were like a giraffe's tail to the Scots . . . over their heads.

Maybe his players were lulled by Mo Johnston's 8th-minute strike when he pounced on an intended pass back, and made the awkward bounce of the ball look easy as he leaned over and rammed in the opener.

Sweeper Dave Narey didn't have the same control when six minutes later he fretted over a bouncing through ball and finally hit it against Koliandris who went on to equalise.

If the Scots were uneasy then, they were positively unnerved two minutes into the second half when Leighton gave away a needless corner and then failed to collect the ball as it came over from the flag.

The scene that followed was one from a school playground as Leighton flapped, defenders flailed, and forwards lashed out till finally Ioannou made the first decisive move in a dozen to slam the ball in the net.

At this moment in time, the thought must have crossed Roxburgh's mind that one of his pre-match utterances had been about the fact that the French had fired coach Henri Michel after a draw in Cyprus.

'A shambles' was his charitable view of the goal. Then Richard the Lionheart set out on his personal crusade. He arrived as back-up man at the edge of the box in the 53rd minute to meet a Johnston flick and angle a deflected shot past the goalkeeper.

When a Johnston volley hit the woodwork towards the end, it looked as though the game was up for Scotland . . . in all respects.

Enter Gough again.

'Even when we were down 2-1 and struggling, I knew we had to do something,' recalls the Ibrox man. 'After I

The Great Escape

Pat Nevin displays his skills at Hampden against Cyprus.

equalised, I felt we could get a winner. I knew it was late when Roy Aitken flighted in the free kick perfectly. I also knew I was going to score when I met it.

'But I certainly didn't realise the game had gone so long. The win was vital for us. We had two home games coming up against France and Cyprus, and knew that if we won them we had a great chance of qualifying.'

However, this was not the last time the Scots were glad to see the back of Cyprus.

By the time the men from the sunshine island made a

Scotland: Five in a Row

return visit to Hampden on April 26, 1989, thousands of Scottish supporters were practising 'Yer Lambrusco's magic' for the forthcoming trip to Italy.

A month earlier a Mo Johnston double had given an inspired Scottish side a 2-0 victory over France and put them top of the section with 7 points out of 8.

Pure dead brilliant. A wee drubbing of the Cypriots would do nicely. Sure hadn't Colin Stein rattled in four as Scotland knocked the moussaka out of the very same lot in an 8-0 win 20 years previously?

This time the Cypriots nearly knocked the haggis out of the Scots, who had much of the play but had to settle thankfully for a 2-1 victory after being pulled back to 1-1 in the second half.

The main highlight was Mo Johnston's brilliant overhead kick in the first half (which he dismissed modestly as a 'lucky strike') which made him Scotland's leading all-time World Cup marksman with eight goals.

A beautifully struck equaliser from Nicolaou in the 63rd minute had the 50,081 crowd anticipating another of those nights of frustration which come along with the Scotland scarf.

Ally McCoist put matters right with a close-in goal.

But the best thing about the night was that the Hillsborough Disaster Fund benefited from the entire gate takings. Plus the players' fees.

Magic Mo-ments

THERE ARE DIFFERING OPINIONS as to what the crucial element was in Scotland's progress to Italy.

Was it luck, in the shape of the famous elastic watch owned by East German referee Siegfried Kirschen which allowed the game against Cyprus to run into nearly six minutes of injury time and Richard Gough snatched a dramatic winner?

Was it the form at Hampden, where we took six points out of eight?

Was it the indifferent form of France who changed manager in mid-campaign and unexpectedly dropped a point away to Cyprus?

Andy Roxburgh believes it was the winning start in Oslo in September 1988 that did the trick.

But what there can be no argument about is that the contribution by striker Maurice Johnston was vital.

Flo-Mo swept past defences right from the start of the campaign.

He scored the winner against Norway in Oslo on September 14, 1988.

He forced the ball over the line in the 1-1 draw with Yugoslavia at Hampden on October 19, 1988.

He rattled in the opener in the dramatic 3-2 win over Cyprus on February 8, 1989 and he dumped France with a double at Hampden on March 8, 1989.

Finally he scored what turned out to be the winner against Cyprus at Hampden on April 6, 1989 with a spectacular overhead kick which had former England striker Malcolm Macdonald comparing him favourably to the legendary Denis Law.

A delighted Mo Johnston and delighted Steve Nicol. Mo has just given Scotland the lead against Yugoslavia at Hampden.

That was five games in a row with goals . . . goals that took Mo to the top as Scotland's leading World Cup marksman with eight goals in all, overhauling both Joe Jordan and Kenny Dalglish.

All this was done while he was a player with Nantes in the French League.

By the summer of 1989 he was a Rangers player, a sensational move that followed a brief waltz with his old partner Celtic before he made the dance an excuse-me and left, opting for the 'jigging' at the ritzy joint across the way.

Mo has lived with pressure all his footballing life: with Partick Thistle, Celtic and Watford it was his rakish lifestyle that caught the public attention.

Magic Mo-ments

People were so taken by the booze and birds image they tended to overlook his ability on the field.

Playing in French football added more intelligence to Johnston's bustling style of play. His work-rate is tremendous, and he does so many important things outside the box that it's hard to see how he manages to get back inside so often to score.

Clearly a mutual admiration society exists between the striker and the Scotland World Cup boss. 'Maurice is always desperately keen to play for Scotland,' says boss Roxburgh. 'His contribution has been immense.'

Roxburgh has given Mo most of his caps . . . and has had his faith in the player repaid over and over.

Of all the games and all the goals, Johnston takes particular pleasure in his two-goal performance which served the *coup de grâce* on the French at Hampden.

'I can go home with a smile on my face,' commented Johnston after the game.

Home being Nantes. But the smile didn't last long, for some of Les Punters in France were not amused at being turfed out of the World Cup club by a player in the French League, and Johnston was the object of some very nasty threats.

The French fury probably did a good turn for Scottish football, for it was only a month or so later that Johnston elected to come back home to Scotland to continue his career.

Probably on the premise that if you're going to get threatening letters, they might as well be in a language you understand!

Johnston's World Cup efforts even brought words of admiration from Manchester United manager Alex Ferguson, the man Mo unhesitatingly dubs 'the man I hate most in the World'.

This dates back to the 1986 World Cup where Ferguson,

Brian McClair, Mo Johnston and Steve Nicol in action against Yugoslavia at Hampden.

Magic Mo - ments

then acting Scottish team boss, axed Johnston from the World Cup pool . . . a move many people believe was crazy.

Including Johnston, who still likes to point out that Scotland's only World Cup goal in Mexico came from midfield man Gordon Strachan.

After Johnston's brace of goals against France, Fergie admitted: 'Johnston is as good as any striker in Britain.

'All he needs now is the platform of the World Cup Finals to show he is genuinely World class.'

Well, Mo has made the greatest football stage of all.

We will see in June whether he can command the spotlight. One thing is for sure . . . he'll be trying.

French manager Michel Platini, who will undoubtedly be buried with his black raincoat draped tastefully over his shoulders — and in a coffin big enough to accommodate one final Gallic shrug — has the final word.

'In France, Johnston learned to play well for Scotland.'

Nightmare Ally

ALLY McCOIST has nightmares about the goal that finally carted Scotland through to the World Cup Finals.

Not about missing the 44th-minute chance. 'I was always confident I was going to score,' says the ebullient Rangers striker.

'When Maurice Malpas headed back a kick-out from the goalkeeper, I was in the clear. The first thing I checked was for offside — but I could see a Norwegian defender to my right so I knew I was OK.

'The next thing was the goalkeeper. I knew he was advancing on me at a rate of knots. But I just timed my arrival right and the lob beat him.

'It was an unbelievable moment. Even then I knew we were in the Finals and that my lifetime ambition had been realised.'

But what Ally didn't realise was just how close he came to being clobbered by the 6ft 3in giant Erik Thorsvedt.

'Every time I look at the goal now on video I shudder,' says Ally.

'I never really looked at Thorsvedt as he came out, I was concentrating on the ball and getting to it first.

'But I'm certainly glad Norway didn't need a point to qualify. Otherwise Thorsvedt might have killed me.

'As it was, his boot couldn't have been that far off my face. And I take enough knocks there as it is.'

McCoist makes his goal sound simple. But it wasn't. It contained speed of action and thought . . . and bravery.

I'll put it this way: if Scotland had been up against a more ruthless nation that the sporting Norwegians . . . like

Nightmare Ally

The goal that sent Scotland to Italy. Ally McCoist scores against Norway at Hampden.

the Italians or Germans, for instance . . . Ally would have paid in pain for his bravery.

McCoist's superb execution of the chance just on the interval set a half-time ceilidh going on the Hampden terracings. The 63,987 fans who filled Hampden on the

Scotland: Five in a Row

evening of Wednesday just KNEW that Scotland were on the way.

'We're going to Italy,' they bellowed all through the second half in true Pavarotti fashion. Even when Fjortoft smacked the post with a 57th-minute shot, the Scots remained on song.

Then the tune got stuck in their throats. It just wouldn't be Scotland without one final piece of drama . . . which came in the shape of a fizzer of a shot from 45 yards by Norwegian defender Erland Johnsen in the dying seconds.

The charitable view taken was that the ball's violent movement in the air — 'it weaved about like an Exocet missile,' explained Andy Roxburgh — flummoxed goalkeeper Jim Leighton.

The less charitable question whether the keeper's late flap at the ball, helping it into the net, was due to the fact he wears contact lenses and didn't see the ball coming at him from all that distance.

In the end it didn't really matter . . . except that everyone was thankful it had come in the dying seconds of the game and not with 15 minutes to go. And also that Scotland didn't need to WIN the game to qualify.

It also prolonged the debate about the inconsistent form shown throughout the World Cup campaign by the Manchester United goalkeeper (more of which later).

At the end of an exhausting 90 minutes, physically and mentally, Andy Roxburgh was as drained as any of his players.

'Anyone have a pacemaker?' was his opening remark to the assembled journalists. The toll taken on his nerve and strength over the eight-game, 14-month trek finally caught up with him.

But it didn't prevent him from making the kind of calm, analytical summary for which he's noted.

'The win over Norway in our very first game 14 months ago set us up. That was the key.

Ally celebrates Scotland's entry to the World Cup Finals.

Scotland: Five in a Row

'Only Scotland and Yugoslavia won there. And we are the two qualifiers.

'The way we got there was not for the faint-hearted. After Ally McCoist's goal there were a lot of drained bodies out on the pitch.' He could include the bench AND the Press Box in that category.

And in the most accurate assessment of all he added: 'When we get to Italy, no one will remember how we got there. The last-minute goal we lost against Norway or the extra-time winner we scored in Cyprus.'

Too right. The tartan army are not looking backwards, they are looking forwards. The scrimping, scraping and conniving to get to Italy — with or without wife and weans — started immediately.

There will be some amazing stories of how they got there. Just to be present when Scotland kicks off the campaign against the unknowns of Costa Rica in the Ferrari Stadium in Genoa on the afternoon of Saturday June 16.

In golf, it's not how but how many that counts. In football, being there is all that matters.

Outgoing S.F.A. secretary Ernie Walker, who has masterminded four of Scotland's World Cup finals appearances, says succinctly: 'When we qualify for the World Cup, everyone in the country walks that little bit taller.'

There will be a lot of 5 ft 4 in giants in Turin and Genoa this summer.

Italy Bound . . . ?

LIKE EVERY OTHER manager before him, and undoubtedly every one to follow, Andy Roxburgh has run into the traditional problems facing all Scottish team bosses:

LACK of co-operation from certain clubs when it comes to releasing players.

LOSS of form of key men at various stages in a season.

LOTS of injuries, some genuine others genuinely mystifying as the victim recovers to play for his club just a few days later.

It was ever so.

In the 1990 campaign, Roxburgh had to contend with the growing criticism of two of his vital players . . . captain Roy Aitken and goalkeeper Jim Leighton.

The rumbles about Aitken started as early as the first qualifying game against Norway, where his leadership qualities were called into question.

The defeats a year later in Yugoslavia and France swelled the wave of discontent, and eventually led to Aitken declaring he had been through enough and wanted to leave Scottish football.

Which he eventually did after a protracted process of transfer wrangling between Celtic and Newcastle.

The Celtic reaction was to blame the popular press for the aggro. But truth be known, it was the football writers of such august journals as the *Glasgow Herald* and the *Sunday Times* who first mooted the prospect of Aitken stepping down.

Anyway, Aitken is now safely ensconced in Newcastle

after his half-million pound deal and appears a more contented man.

He has every intention of leading Scotland in the World Cup.

'I don't want to talk about the past', he says, 'Just the future. I have been lucky enough to become one of the select few players who have won more than 50 caps for their country.

'I led Scotland to Italy. I want to keep on doing it'.

Similarly, keeper Jim Leighton became an increasingly targeted figure. He was indicted for at least one of the goals in the nerve-wracking 3-2 win over Cyprus.

He recovered some status with a fine display against France at Hampden . . . but the finger of suspicion was directed again after the heavy defeats in Zagreb and Paris.

And since he is playing in a struggling Manchester United team, behind an unsettled defence, his every error is under scrutiny.

All of this has left Andy Roxburgh in a dilemma: does he ignore form, and go for experience?

Leighton has become Scotland's most capped goalkeeper, and the only way his deputy Andy Goram could gain any real experience would be to be given the job in the warm-up games leading to Italy.

Even then, Goram would still be well short in the big-match feel.

Aitken and Leighton have well over 100 caps between them. Vital experience.

Yet people point to the mistaken loyalty shown by Ally MacLeod in the 1978 World Cup where he stuck by players like Bruce Rioch and Don Masson . . . only to discover they no longer had the legs to do the job.

Mind you, Scotland were not helped in this instance by the fact that both Masson and Rioch, who were with Derby, had been dropped by former national manager Tommy

Italy bound . . . ?

Jim Leighton is beaten in Oslo for Norway's only goal.

Docherty who arrived at the Baseball Ground to describe the pair as 'poor buys'. Not exactly morale-boosting stuff.

Roxburgh picked Aitken for every international from the day he took over in September 1986 until the final qualifying game against Norway some 25 matches later.

Ready replacements for a player of Aitken's stature and experience do not abound in Scottish football. Roxburgh should stand by his man.

The men who will carry Scottish dreams into Italy will come from the following list:

Goalkeepers

Jim Leighton, 31. Made over 300 League appearances with Aberdeen and won every honour at Pittodrie under manager Alex Ferguson. Followed his boss south in 1986 in a £700,000 move. Won his first cap against East Germany in October 1982 and his 50th against Cyprus at Hampden on April 26, 1989. 6 ft 1 in, 12 st 8 lb.

Andy Goram, 26. Joined Hibs from Oldham in 1987 for £350,000. Has become a great favourite and team captain.

Scotland: Five in a Row

Born in Bury, he is a top-class cricketer. Six caps. 5 ft 11 in, 12 st 12 lb.

Bryan Gunn, 26. Was Jim Leighton's understudy at Pittodrie for many years before moving to Norwich where he has been automatic first team choice for the English first division side. 6 ft 2 in, 13 st 13 lb.

Defenders

Richard Gough, 28. Forty-four caps. Born in Stockholm, brought up in South Africa but a dedicated Scottish internationalist. Was with Rangers as a teenager, moved on to Dundee United who developed him into a top-class defender then sold him to Tottenham for £750,000 . . . who sold him back to Rangers a year later for twice that amount. A scorer of vital goals, none more so than his double against Cyprus last year. 6 ft, 11 st 12 lb.

Stewart McKimmie, 27. Joined up at Pittodrie in 1983 from Dundee. Pacy, good tackling full back who has won full caps against England and Chile last year. 5 ft 8 in, 10 st 7 lb.

Steve Clarke, 26. Ayrshire born defender who started his career with St Mirren where he played more than 150 League games before being transferred to Chelsea three years ago for £400,000. Has five caps. Can play either full back position or central defence. 5 ft 9 in, 11 st 2 lb.

Alex McLeish, 31. Scotland's most capped defender with 66 honours, and second behind Kenny Dalglish in the all-time listings. Big, aggressive red-haired central defender who gives 100 per cent every time. The Aberdeen defender is 6 ft 1 in and 12 st 4 lb.

Willie Miller, 35. Has amassed 65 caps over a long career, many of them in partnership with his Pittodrie team-mate McLeish. Rated the best penalty-box tackler in the business. Has won all the honours with the Dons, and is still looking for more. Played in Scotland's last two World Cup campaigns. 5 ft 10½ in, 11 st 8 lb.

Italy Bound . . . ?

On World Cup business at Zagreb, Yugoslavia, Scotland stalwarts Alex McLeish and the unfortunate Steve Nicol who gave away an own goal.

Gary Gillespie, 29. Talented central defender who carries the ball well out of defence. Injury has been a problem for this former Falkirk player who was transferred from Coventry to Liverpool four seasons ago. Should have had more than seven caps but for his injury problems. 6 ft 2 in, 12 st 7 lb.

Maurice Malpas, 27. The most consistent defender in Scotland who seldom turns in a bad game for Dundee United or his country. Club captain, and tipped as a future Scotland leader. Great reader of the game and a sound tackler. 31 caps. 5 ft 8 in, 10 st 11 lb.

Scotland: Five in a Row

Derek Whyte, 21. This rising young Celtic star has won two caps against Belgium and Bulgaria as a substitute, but more will follow when he gains experience. A Celtic first team regular despite his youth, and has won League and Cup medals. 5 ft 11 in, 11 st 5 lb.

Craig Levein, 25. His return to first-class football after nearly a year out because of a bad knee injury has been welcomed by all fans. A solid tackler and good user of the ball. Joined Hearts from Cowdenbeath in 1983. 6 ft, 11 st, 4 lb.

Davie McPherson, 26. Three caps. The giant Hearts defender was brought in by Scotland for the vital final qualifying game against Norway for his third cap and did the job expected. Formerly with Rangers, he was sold to Hearts for £300,000 . . . and they have never regretted the deal. 6 ft 3 in, 12 st.

Midfield

Stuart McCall, 25. Yorkshire born with Scottish parents, this dynamic little midfielder started his career with Bradford where he played 238 League games and scored 37 goals before moving in a big-money deal to Everton. Has won under-21 honours, but still waiting for his first top cap. 5 ft 6 in, 10 st 11lb.

Murdo Macleod, 31. 12 caps. Battling midfielder who can also turn out at full back. Began his career with Dumbarton, was transferred for £100,000 to Celtic where he was a midfield grafter for many years. His move to German football several years ago was a surprise — but he has taken to soccer life well with Borussia Dortmund. 5 ft 8 in, 11 st.

Gary McAllister, 25. This talented Leicester youngster could have made a £1 million move by the time the World Cup Finals are played. Started his career with Motherwell before moving south. He is wanted by many clubs, including Notts Forest and Celtic. Could go abroad. 5 ft 10 in, 9 st 7 lb.

Andy Goram, Hibs, hopes to make the Scottish team this summer.

Steve Nicol, 28. Mr Versatile, who turns in a good performance in defence or midfield. Former Ayr United player who has become indispensable for Liverpool since his £100,000 transfer five years ago. Player of the Year in England in 1989. 23 caps. 5 ft 10 in, 12 st.

Roy Aitken, 31. 50 caps. Roy ended a long career with Celtic, boy and man, to move to Newcastle in a £500,000 deal this year. Driving, commanding player with a direct approach to everything. Club and country captain. 6 ft, 13 st.

Paul McStay, 25. Has succeeded Aitken to the captaincy of Celtic, the club for which he has starred since a 17-year-old. Won honours at all levels and has 41 full caps. A wonderful touch footballer with great vision. Packs a powerful shot, but is too reluctant to display it. 5 ft 10 in, 10 st 7 lb.

Jim Bett, 30. One of the most experienced players in the Scottish team, having played for Airdrie, Dundee, Belgium club Lokeren, Rangers and now Aberdeen, as well as a spell in Iceland. Has won 22 caps, and his performance in the final qualifying game against Norway was out-standing. 5 ft 11½ in, 12 st 3 lb.

John Collins, 22. This Hibs youngster has won a full cap against Saudi Arabia, and more are sure to follow. Quick, aggressive player who can make and take goals. 5 ft 7 in, 9 st 10 lb.

Forwards

Brian McClair, 26. Former Celtic striker who moved south to Manchester United for a near £1 million deal three years ago. Can also operate in midfield. Prolific scorer with Motherwell, his first club, and Celtic, and had a good first couple of seasons at Old Trafford. 13 caps. 5 ft 9 in, 12 st 2 lb.

Maurice Johnston, 27. Mo is one of football's most controversial characters, the culmination of which was his transfer last year from French club Nantes to Rangers after seemingly being set to rejoin Celtic. Former Patrick Thistle and Watford striker, he has featured in transfer deals totalling more than £3 million. Has 30 caps. Scored a series of vital goals in Scotland's qualifying run, including both in the 2-0 win over France at Hampden. 5 ft 10 in, 11 st.

Italy Bound . . . ?

Dave McPherson, Hearts, in World Cup action against Cyprus.

Scotland: Five in a Row

Ally McCoist, 27. The other half of a striking partnership that is doing great business for club and country. One of the game's most likeable extroverts, he started his career with St Johnstone, turned down Rangers to join Sunderland and then two seasons later did arrive at Ibrox. Prolific scorer, he is now the leading Premier marksman and has become Rangers' post-war record holder for League goals, overtaking Derek Johnstone's 131 mark. Twenty caps. 5 ft 10 in, 12 st.

Gordon Durie, 24. Injury has hampered the club and country career of this stocky striker. Began his career with East Fife where he scored 26 goals in 81 League games. That got him a move to Hibs where he netted 14 goals in his 47 League appearances. He was then sold to Chelsea where he netted 34 times in his first 84 League games. Only four caps because of his injury troubles in the past year. 6 ft, 12 st.

Alan McInally, 27. Rambo, as he was quickly dubbed at Celtic Park after a £100,000 transfer from Ayr United, is a big rangy striker who runs directly at the opposition. Scored 17 goals in 65 League games for Celtic, but was sold off to Aston Villa where he lasted less than two seasons but managed 18 goals in 58 League games. He was then off on a £1.1 million deal to German club Bayern Munich last summer. Has four caps. 6 ft 1 in, 13 st 3 lb.

Davie Cooper, 34. One of the most talented players in Scottish football in the past decade. Won every honour in his long career with Rangers and is now enjoying a new lease of soccer life with home-town Motherwell. No-one passes a ball better or hits a dead ball with such accuracy. 15 caps. 5 ft 8½ in, 12 st 5 lb.

Eric Black, 26. The former Aberdeen striker is currently based in French football with Metz. A prolific scorer, he is particularly potent in the air. But also troubled by injuries

Italy Bound . . . ?

John Collins, Hibs, tipped by many to star in Italy.

to his back. Was called into the Scotland squad for the pre-World Cup visit to Genoa. Has won two caps as substitute against Hungary and Luxembourg in 1988.

Pat Nevin, 25. Has eight caps. This tricky little winger is an old-fashioned type of player who likes to have the ball at his feet and run at defences. Twists and turns quickly. Started his career with Clyde, moved on to Chelsea where he played 193 League games and scored 36 goals before a near £1 million transfer to Everton. 5 ft 6 in, 10 st.

Robert Fleck, 26. The stocky, aggressive style of ex-Rangers man Fleck has won him a host of admirers at Norwich. He's a tough man to play against, as many of England's top defenders have discovered. Scored 29 goals in 85 League games for Rangers in partnership with Ally McCoist. Netted 17 times in his first 51 League matches for Norwich. Under 21 cap. 5 ft 8 in, 11 st 8 lb.

Scotland: Five in a Row

Davie Cooper, Motherwell, with a wealth of international experience, recently re-introduced into the Scottish squad.

Costa What?

COSTA WHAT? That was the first reaction among Scots when the draw in Rome on December 10 brought the name of Costa Rica out in the section alongside Brazil and Sweden.

Nothing was known of the little Central American country: not where it lay; not the population and certainly not the football pedigree.

'Costa Rica are the last great mystery,' said Scotland boss Andy Roxburgh after he had watched Brazil in a friendly against Holland, 'I must find out about them.'

And with the efficient organisation that is his trademark, he set about putting that right.

So did the Scottish press. Within days we learned that Costa Rica had a population of less than half of Scotland.

That the country is poor. The footballers are heroes but don't earn much. That it lies between Panama and Nicaragua, which is hardly the most peaceful zone in the World.

Coffeee, bananas, sugar and beef are the main products. Not footballers, so far.

But it has produced a Nobel Peace Prize winner. President Oscar Arias Sanchez won that prestigious award for his efforts in helping secure peace in neighbouring Nicaragua.

There *is* no footballing pedigree to talk of in Costa Rica. Just the usual Latin love of the game and fiery reaction if things don't go right. Mind you, nothing has ever quite been as bad as the reaction by El Salvador at losing an international to Honduras back in the 1980s; They were so mad they declared war and invaded!

Scotland: Five in a Row

Costa Rica have had their moments, too, like the near riot that followed their victory in the qualifying games against El Salvador, who seem to be particularly sore losers. But never before have they qualified for the World Cup Finals.

They were undoubtedly helped along the way by the fact that Mexico, always the strongest side in the Concacaf group, had been disqualified from entry for the World Cup by F.I.F.A.

That brought the entry down to 15 teams, and Costa Rica had to play 10 games to make it through instead of a dozen.

Their record of games reads:

First Round
17.7.88	Costa Rica 1	Panama 1
31.7.88	Panama 0	Costa Rica 2

Second Round
Costa Rica given a bye because of their two games against Mexico were cancelled when the Mexicans were disqualified.

Third Round
19.3.89	Guatemala 1	Costa Rica 0
2.4.89	Costa Rica 2	Guatemala 1
16.4.89	Costa Rica 1	USA 0
30.4.89	USA 1	Costa Rica 0
28.5.89	Trinidad/Tobago 1	Costa Rica 1
11.6.89	Costa Rica 1	Trinidad/Tobago 0
25.6.89	El Salvador 2	Costa Rica 4
16.7.89	Costa Rica 1	El Salvador 0

The Costa Ricans had played 10 games, won six, drawn two and lost two. They scored 13 goals in the 10 games and conceded 7.

Costa What?

Their final victory over El Salvador on 16 July 1989 left them at the top of the final qualifying table with 11 points.

But they were not guaranteed to be through at that stage. They could still be caught by both USA and Trinidad/Tobago.

The Yanks had still four games to play by the time Costa Rica had finished their programme. If they won them all, they would finish up with 13 points. They could even afford to drop a point and still finish ahead of Costa Rica.

Trinidad and Tobago were similarly placed, and indeed had five games left to go when the Costa Ricans wrapped up their schedule.

Costa Rica were sitting on the points. They were also sitting on a perch that could be blasted out from under them.

You couldn't hear in San José, capital of Costa Rica, for the rattle of the prayer beads. And the prayers worked.

Both T and T and America dropped vital points, the USA in particular slipping up badly at home against El Salvador in a goal-less draw.

And when it became clear they couldn't be caught, Costa Rica staged one of the biggest parties the country had ever seen.

The Ticos — as the Costa Ricans like to call themselves — were dancing in the streets for days.

When the party was over, Costa Rica set about preparing for Italy. They players are national heroes, and will earn sums far beyond the reach of the ordinary man.

But they will be by no means rich. The Costa Rican F.A. just doesn't have the cash.

They are helped by donations from the population, and by sponsorship. Indeed, the winning goal in their final game against El Salvador was incorporated into a petrol advert on TV . . . and shown every 15 minutes.

Scotland: Five in a Row

The scorer, Pastor Fernandez, was playing in his first international and became an immediate national hero.

It would be easy to write off the Costa Ricans, because of their lack of World Cup standing and the general low rating of the Central American countries.

Many people have already. The USA in particular have given them no high rating . . . despite the fact that the Ticos finished above them in the qualifying group.

'You will hammer them' was the emphatic message from midfield man John Harkes. 'Scotland should take them apart'.

Maybe since John's parents are Scots who emigrated to New Jersey, this might just have something to do with his favourable verdict.

The fact that the Costa Rica national squad toured in Europe last autumn with a marked lack of success, also tends to build up a false sense of security.

They lost to A.S. Roma and Verona in Italy and Dukla Prague in Czechoslovakia. They did however record a victory over Italian Third Division side Nuova Rigor.

But in Andy Roxburgh's book (and video recorder) no news is not good news.

There are going to be no surprises for Scotland by the time the teams line up in Genoa on 11 June.

The lessons of Peru in 1978, when Scotland strolled unprepared into a mini-blitz, have never been forgotten up at S.F.A. headquarters.

Scotland may never be the best; but we can at least be the best prepared.

Iran, Zaire and New Zealand are names from past World Cup campaigns that are also remembered. There are no push-overs, as Scotland should well recall.

Roxburgh knows this from present experience. He has watched his team draw against Luxembourg, Saudia Arabia and Malta and suffered the stinging criticism which follows every time the Scots fail to land a minnow.

Costa What?

Costa Rica would not be allowed to remain the great unknown for long.

Which is why he set out like Christopher Columbus to discover for himself — in America naturally.

And it's a good job he did a 'see for yourself' stint in Miami where the Ticos were playing in a tournament against USA and Uruguay.

For if he had relied on the conflicting views of other people, he would still be wondering.

Swedish coach Olle Nordin has dismissed the Ticos. 'I see no problem' he declares in the best Nelson tradition.

But Yugoslavian, Blagoje Vidinic, who was coach of Zaire when Scotland played in the 1974 World Cup, warns: 'Andy Roxburgh should not write off the threat they pose.'

You pays your money . . . or, in Andy's case, the S.F.A. does it for him . . . and you makes your own choice.

Roxburgh went, saw . . . and was convinced. 'They were much better than I expected. They showed more class and quality than I anticipated.

'They have players who would give any defence a hard time'.

They also have a player who is expected to be hard on everyone. Bearded Alvano Solano has been described by US coach Bob Gansler as 'a man who takes no prisoners'.

But it wasn't the hard man, but the hit men, who impressed Andy Roxburgh.

Strikers Evaristo Coronado and the lanky Hernan Medford are keen and able. And pacy.

And the luck of the draw which has given the Scots the Ticos in the opening game on June 11 means that Costa Rica will not only be fresh, they will be all out to strut their stuff in front of the world audience for the first time.

If Scotland know a little about the Central American side, they know less about the Scots.

Scotland: Five in a Row

'I expect we will watch them on video nearer the time' commented skipper Roger Flores.

They have not, apparently, heard of Mo Johnston or Ally McCoist. Genoa could sort that out.

The majority of the eight clubs which make up the League competition in Costa Rica are based in the capital, San Jose.

Players earn under £80 a week plus one or two perks.

The country's F.A., like the nation, is strapped for cash and the players who were promised more than £4,000 a man for qualifying were getting a bit twitchy when months later there was no sign of the dinero.

All seems to be settled now.

The country's leading player is midfieler Juan Cayasso, scorer of 16 goals in his first 32 internationals for his country.

And striker Claudio Jara, an experienced 30-year-old scored some vital qualifying goals for his country.

Most of the World Cup squad is drawn from just a few clubs.

Leading team Saprissa will supply anything up to eight of the squad, which has that team's supporters claiming *they* are the World Cup side.

Cartagines, Herediano and Alajuelense are the other major suppliers.

There was a major British influence on Costa Rican football in the early days . . . maybe that's why they play in red, white and blue! . . . and indeed at one point had a competition (now disbanded) called the Great Britain Cup.

The Costa Rican side is like so many of the Latin line: speedy, excitable, with good control of everything except their temper.

If things are going well, good and well. When things go bad — they get mad. Scotland could be in for a hot summer's evening on 11 June.

Costa What?

The side the Scots will face will come from the following players:

Goalkeepers

Luis Cornejo, 30. An agile, brave goalkeeper from the Ramonese club.

Jorge Hidalgo, 23. Plays for Herediano.

Hector Barrantes, 25. From the Municipal Puntarenas club who made the national squad only last year.

Defenders

Enrique Diaz, 31. Plays for Deportivo Saprissa. Was in the 1984 Olympic team.

Vladimir Queseda, 25. Saprissa. Comes from a famous footballing family and has been a regular in the squad in recent years.

Mauricio Montero, 26. From the Alajuelense club. Rated one of their best players. Missed a penalty in the 1-0 qualifying defeat against US.

José Carlos Chavez, 31. Club-mate of Montero at Alajuelense.

Marvin Obando, 31. Herediano and Tomas Segura a 27-year-old from Saprissa are also candidates.

Midfield

German Chavarria, 31. Herediano. Played for his country in the Los Angeles Olympics.

Juan Cayasso, 29. Saprissa. Country's most capped player and another Olympic man.

Oscar Ramirez, 25. Alajuelense. Is expected to make a move to Spanish football after the World Cup.

Carlos Hidalgo, 26. Suprissa. Unpredictable, but dangerous when he's in the mood.

Marvin Obando, 30. Herediano. The Steve Nicol of Costa Rica. Can play in any position from central defence through to attack.

Alvaro Sclano, 29. Alajuelense. The hatchet man of the side according to the US team. Another Olympic squad man.

Hector Marachena, 25. Cartagines. An ever-present in the squad for the past year or so. Strong tackler.

Forwards

Leoni Flores, 25. Puntarenas. Made the national last year and scored two goals in the 4-2 win over El Salvador which sparked a mini-riot.

Evaristo Cornonado, 29. Saprissa. A player Andy Roxburgh noted as a danger man. Another member of the 1984 Olympic squad.

Luis Jara, 30. Herediano. Can operate in midfield as well. Packs a powerful long-range shot and is a free kick specialist.

Gilberto Rohden, 27. Alajuelense. Can operate on either wing.

Hernan Medford, 22. Saprissa. Tall, athletic player with a fine turn of speed. Marked out as a threat by Andy Roxburgh.

Pastor Fernandez, 26. Newcomer to the squad, but made his name by scoring the goal in the 1-0 victory over El Salvador which gave his country a World Cup place for the first time.

Read all about . . . Sweden

THERE ARE MANY PEOPLE who feel inclined to write Sweden off in the World Cup.

Scotland can forget this idea . . . since many of the dismissal notices have come from England, despite the fact that the English finished runners-up behind the Swedes in their qualifying group.

Coach Olle Nordin certainly does have a squad on his hands that is full of players who are . . . well, mature.

Midfieler Glenn Stromberg is 30 . . . Former Rangers man Robert Prytz is the same age.

Defender Peter Larsson will be 30 by the time he gets to Italy and the Ravelli twins (goalkeeper Thomas and defender Andreas) are both a year or so past the 30 mark.

But old doesn't necessarily mean decrepit, and there will be many moments in Italy where experience will triumph over youth.

For many of the Swedish stars this will be a last World Cup fling — and they intend to make it a good one.

Indeed, their coach Nordin is convinced his side will take at least second place in the section, and that 'Scotland's best chance of making the next phase is as one of the four third placed sides who will get through'.

He sees no reason to fear the Scots — or the Scottish style of play.

For Sweden's game has been developed along British lines ever since Englishman George Raynor gave up his post as reserve team trainer at Aldershot just after the last war and took over as boss of the Swedish international side.

Scotland: Five in a Row

George was from Yorkshire, but the Swedes clearly got the message.

By 1950 he had organised them well enough for the Swedes to battle through their section games in the Finals in Brazil to finish up in third place (despite a 7-1 hammering from Brazil along the way).

Eight years later they improved on that third place.

They were the hosts in 1958, and they made the most of home advantage. Wins over Mexico (3-0), Hungary (2-1), Russia (2-0) and West Germany (3-1) carried them through to the Final.

Unfortunately for them, they had another bad experience at the hands of the boys from Brazil . . . one boy in particular — Pele.

He scored twice as the South Americans romped to a 5-2 victory, including the goal that I personally rate as probably the greatest of all time. I can still picture the way he took a pass on his chest, dropped it onto his knee, flicked it over a defender's head, ran round his opponent and volleyed the ball into the net.

Genius is spelled P.E.L.E.

Sweden's group two success in their qualifying run means their eighth appearance in the World Cup Final stages.

The group two games went like this:

19.10.88	England	0	Sweden	0
5.11.88	Albania	1	Sweden	2
8. 3.89	Albania	0	England	2
26. 4.89	England	5	Albania	0
7. 5.89	Sweden	2	Poland	1
3. 6.89	England	3	Poland	0
8.10.89	Sweden	3	Albania	1
11.10.89	Poland	0	England	0
25.10.89	Poland	0	Sweden	2
15.11.89	Albania	1	Poland	2

Read all about . . . Sweden

This gave a final group table reading of:

	P	W	D	L	F	A	Pts
Sweden	6	4	2	0	9	3	10
England	6	3	3	0	10	0	9
Poland	6	2	1	3	4	8	5
Albania	6	0	0	6	3	15	0

When the draw in Rome on December 10 put the Swedes into the same Group C as Scotland, the hype started.

'Scotland have no chance of beating us', announced tough defender Glenn Hysen, who now earns his corn and kroner in British football with Liverpool.

Another in the Swedish over-30s club, age doesn't seem to be bothering Glenn in the competitive heat of the English First Division.

And it is of great Liverpool Scots that he speaks when he compares the current Scotland squad with the sides of the past:

'You have no player in the same class as Kenny Dalglish or Graeme Souness. We still respect Scotland, but I see no reason to fear them.'

Hysen cost Liverpool £600,000 last year from Italian club Fiorentina. So he knows Italy and the scene there well.

So does his national team-mate Johnny Ekstrom, who is now in French football with Cannes but starred with Italian side Empoli for several years.

Like Hysen he thinks it is a lucky break for Sweden that they have landed section minnows Costa Rica in the final game of the Group.

'They should be down and out by then, and looking to going home,' he says.

However, Scotland's chances of a success against the Swedes are given a good rating by one of Celtic's Polish imports, Darek Wdowczyk.

Mats Magnusson, a forward with Benfica eludes a challenge in a Champion's Cup game against Honved.

Read all about . . . Sweden

He skippered the Polish side in both World Cup qualifying games against the Swedes: and despite being on the losing side both times fancies Scotland to mash the Swedes.

'They have defensive faults which Scotland will punish' he says. 'And the goalkeeper Thomas Ravelli clowns around a lot.'

But then he adds warningly: 'They have two powerful strikers in Mats Magnusson and Johnny Ekstrom. They will take a bit of stopping.'

Under the direction of coach Olle Nordin, Sweden have built up an impressive international record.

In the first 36 games under his control they won 20 times, drew 10 and lost only six . . . almost as good a record as anything produced by Abba!

In the process, they have beaten Brazil (2-1 in a tournament in Denmark) and won a four-team tournament featuring Argentina, Russia and West Germany.

Hardly the form of the over-the-hill mob, as some critics are trying to label them.

Sweden, with a population of just over eight million, is like Scotland in many ways: for a start many of their players move to other parts to further their future.

And the Swedish F.A. welcomes the £2 million boost that comes from taking part in the Finals. They missed out in the 1982 and 1986 Finals, and the loss of revenue was a sore blow.

Mind you, their pride was given a Scandinavian skelp last year when they were given a 6-0 walloping by arch rivals Denmark, the biggest defeat of the century for the Swedes. But since it was a game to help mark the Danish F.A. centenary, maybe the Swedes were just being kind to their hosts!

When the time comes to summon the Swedish mercenaries home for the World Cup preparations, the bugle will have to be sounded all over Europe.

Scotland: Five in a Row

Hysen is in England, Ekstrom in France. But that's just part of the Swedish foreign legion.

PORTUGAL is where big striker Mats Magnusson operates. This 26-year-old, formerly with Malmo and Servette of Switzerland, is currently with Benfica who rely a lot on his power in the air and skill on the ground.

Alongside him in the Benfica line-up is Sweden's most expensive export, Jonas Thern. It cost Benfica a record £950,000 to sign this 23-year-old midfield man from Malmo last summer.

HOLLAND is the base for another two Swedish stars . . . Peter Larsson and Stefan Pettersson.

Larsson is a central defender who turned out for the Rest of the World in the English League Centenary match three years ago. Pettersson is a striker, formerly with IFK Gothenburg. Like so many talented front men he has found his career interrupted by the injuries that come with the job of being 'in there where it hurts'.

SWITZERLAND and Young Boys of Berne is where full back Roger Ljung, 24, plies his trade after moving on from Malmo. Former member of the Swedish Olympic squad.

ITALY boasts a Swedish trio . . . veteran midfielder Glenn Stromberg (30) has won more than 50 caps and is still turning in fine performances for Atalanta.

A former colleague at Atalanta was ex-Rangers midfield man, Robert Prytz, now 31. Prytz, married to a Scots girl with two children born in Scotland, has moved to the fringe of the Swedish squad but his 'insider' knowledge of Scottish football could see him recalled. He also played in Switzerland and Germany.

Anders Limpar is a 24-year-old midfielder with Cremonese having served some time with Young Boys of Berne.

NORWAY tempted full back Dennis Schiller for a short trip across Scandinavia. This 25-year-old is with Lillestroem

Read all about . . . Sweden

and it was only after the move out of Sweden that his cap prospects improved.

The home-based Swedes who could line up against Scotland include twins Thomas and Andreas Ravelli.

Thomas is the No. 1 choice keeper, having moved from Osters Vaxjo last year to join IFK.

The Swedish squad will almost certainly include the following list of players.

Goalkeepers:

Thomas Ravelli, 30. IFK Gothenburg
Sven Andersson, 26. Orgryte

Defenders:

Roland Nilsson, 26. IFK Gothenburg
Sulo Vaatovaara, 27. Norrkoping
Dennis Schiller, 25. Lillestroem
Roger Ljung, 24. Young Boys Berne
Glenn Hysen, 31. Liverpool
Peter Larsson, 29. Ajax Amsterdam
Peter Lonn, 22. Norkopping
Andreas Ravelli, 30. Osters Vaxjo

Midfield:

Glenn Stromberg, 30. Atalanta
Robert Prytz, 31. Atalanta
Klas Ingesson, 24. Malmo
Jonas Thern, 23. Benfica
Stefan Rehn, 23. Everton
Anders Limpar, 24. Cremonese

Forwards:

Mats Magnusson, 26. Benfica
Johnny Ekstrom, 25. Cannes
Jan Hellstrom, 30. Norkopping
Stefan Petterson, 27. Ajax

Scotland: Five in a Row

When Scotland line up against the Swedes in Genoa on June 16, it will be the seventh meeting in history between the teams.

And the good news is that the record reads in Scotland's favour. They have won three, drawn one and lost two of the previous six games.

The first four encounters were in friendly games. More significant is the fact that Scotland handed out a World Cup K.O. to the Swedes in the 1982 qualifying games.

Wee Gordon Strachan was the hero when the Scots opened up their qualifying campaign in Scotkhold on Wednesday, September 10, 1980.

Sweden up to that point had not been defeated at home for 15 years in a World Cup tie. But in the 72nd minute Strachan worked an intricate 1-2 with Archie Gemmill, cut in from the wing and fired a low show into the net for the only goal of the game.

Strachan, of course, figured in Scotland's recent World Cup qualifying battles and other survivors from Stockholm are Aberdeen pair Alex McLeish and Willie Miller.

By the time the countries met in the return match at Hampden a year later, there were many changes in the Swedish line-up.

In came names that the Scots will see again this summer . . . the Ravelli twins, Hysen and Larsson.

But again Scotland prevailed. The recalled Joe Jordan, then playing for A.C. Milan in Italy, scored with a scorching header from a John Robertson free kick in the 20th minute.

Then, seven minutes from time, substitute Andy Gray, brought on for Kenny Dalglish, went down in the box. 'Dive', said the Swedes. 'Penalty', said the Swiss referee.

And wee John Robertson perfomed his normal immaculate job from the spot to tie up a 2-0 victory.

The fact that the Swedes still have four of the team on

duty nine years on is certainly a pointer to the ageing quality of their side. For Scotland, only Alex McLeish is a survivor.

The Scottish side that night was: Rough; McGrain, F. Gray; Wark, McLeish, Hansen; Provan, Dalglish (Gray), Jordan, Hartford, Robertson.

Scotland's full list of meetings with Sweden reads:

1952 (Stockholm, friendly): Sweden 3 Scotland 1 (Liddell).

1953 (Hampden, friendly): Scotland 1 (Johnstone) Sweden 2.

1975 (Gothenburg, friendly): Sweden 1 Scotland 1 (MacDougall)

1977 (Hampden, friendly): Scotland 3 (Hartford, Dalglish, Craig) Sweden 1.

1980 (Stockholm, W.C.) Sweden 0 Scotland 1 (Strachan).

1981 (Hampden, W.C.) Scotland 2 (Jordan, Robertson pen) Sweden 0.

Brazil add a bit of beef

LONG BEFORE WORLD CUP qualifying games ever began two years ago, everyone knew who the 1990 favourites would be . . . Brazil.

Just as everyone predicted that the Final would be between the South Americans and host country Italy.

That's the game the Italian fans are expecting in Rome on the night of July 8.

If it does happen, the boys from Brazil (Class of 1990) will be a different breed from the samba-smooth stars who danced their way into the hearts of the world's soccer fans with victories in 1958, 1962 and 1972.

Elimination in the second stage in Spain in 1982 and the quarter-finals in Mexico the last time, set the idea going in Brazil that they might have to add steel toe caps to the dancing shoes.

This notion was confirmed in 1989 when they came to Europe on tour and had a disastrous time.

They lost 2-1 to Sweden, and even worse were drubbed 4-0 by Denmark.

The Brazilian fan is not at all accustomed to this kind of drubbing: the answer was obvious . . . sack the manager.

But team boss Sebastiano Lazaroni dodged the axe by rightly pointing out that it was a weakened team which toured; he didn't want to go in the first place and the hasty preparations left him with no time to get his men ready.

'It will be different for Italy,' he says. 'All my home players will be released by their clubs and will spend 45 days preparing.'

Brazil add a bit of beef

Ricardo Branco of Brazil in a tussle with Kieft of Holland in a friendly played at Rotterdam.

Scotland: Five in a Row

However, he acknowledges that he will not have his European-based players for all that time.

They will come later: they will also come armed with insight and knowledge which will be incorporated into Brazil's make up.

The Beautiful Game, as they like to call it in Brazil, will be beefed up.

'We must learn from the Italians and the Argentinians. They play well enough to win World Cups. But they also play a physical game if it is needed.'

Which must surely make it clear that it was not just for financial reasons the Brazilians have dispatched 'missionaries' abroad.

When the Brazilians gather in Rio in May, these missionaries will arrive back from Germany, Italy, Portugal, Spain, Holland and France prepared to spread the hot gospel.

Careco, Alemao and Dunga know all about the Italian job, playing as they do for Napoli and Fiorentina.

Aldair and Valdo are in Portugal with Benfica, while the brilliant left-footed Branco is a star with Porto.

Defenders Jorginho and Mozer have been toughened up with Leverkusen in West Germany and Marseilles in France.

And striker Romario has been banging the ball into Dutch nets with PSV Eindhoven at an impressive rate.

Since the poor tour in Europe, coach Lazaroni has steered his team to victory in the South American championships for the first time in 40 years, beating World Cup holders Argentina and the muscle-men of Uruguay.

And in December they came back to Europe to show what they had learned.

They beat Italy 1-0 in an exhibition game in Bologna and then Careca headed them to a 1-0 win over Holland.

They learn quickly, the Brazilians do!

Brazil add a bit of beef

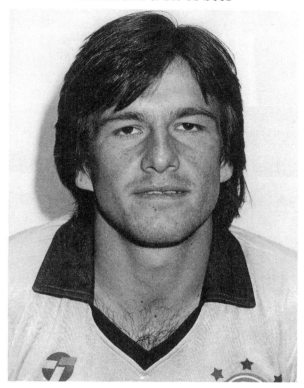

Dungu, a talented midfield player. Look out for him against Scotland.

Scotland: Five in a Row

Manager Lazaroni has opted for a five-man defensive formation, with a sweeper operating just like the Italians.

The two candidates for this vital role are Galvao of the Botofoga club in Rio . . . and the French-based Mozer of Marseilles. It was Mozer who played against Holland and this tall all-round player showed both pace and skill. As well as that wee drop of the hard stuff which Brazil are growing to like.

After their South American Cup success, in which they didn't lose a goal, they went on to play four World Cup qualifying games and conceded only one goal.

That was in a 1-1 draw against Chile in Santiago in August 1989. But it was the return match between these two traditional rivals that brought football one of its most bizarre events for a long time.

Brazil were leading 1-0 in the match at the famous Maracana Stadium on September 3, 1989 when trouble flared. Literally.

A woman fan let loose a celebratory flare which landed close to Chilean goalkeeper Rojas . . . who promptly keeled over claiming he had been hit.

The Chileans walked off the field, and tried to claim the match.

But in the investigation that followed, F.I.F.A. found that the goalkeeper had faked the whole thing and was then aided and abetted by officials.

Result: a life-time ban for Rojas and the Chilean president, plus sundry other hard sentences on various officials and Brazil were awarded a 2-0 victory.

Most importantly of all, Chile will not be allowed to take part in the 1994 World Cup in the United States.

Dramatic stuff, even by South American standards.

The full list of games in the South American Group Two reads:

Brazil add a bit of beef

30.7.89	Venezuela 0 Brazil 4
6.8.89	Venezuela 1 Chile 3
13.8.89	Chile 1 Brazil 1
20.8.89	Brazil 6 Venezuela 0
27.8.89	Chile 5 Venezuela 0
3.9.89	Brazil 2 Chile 0.

The final placings (forgetting the forfeit of the game by Chile) were:

	P	W	D	L	F	A	Pts
Brazil	4	3	1	0	13	1	7
Chile	4	2	1	1	9	4	5
Venezuela	4	0	0	4	1	18	0

By the time they had finished up their game against Holland, the Brazilians had stretched their unbeaten run of games to 16 and conceded just one goal in their last 14 games.

Coach Lazaroni seems to have got the sequence right: don't give anything away and score as often as you can.

Not bad for a failed goalkeeper who never got beyond Second Division football in Brazil. Just goes to confirm a widely held theory that you don't have to be a great player to become a great manager.

With a bit of luck, Andy Roxburgh might easily fall into that category!

The feeling as Brazil march towards the Finals, is that they might be a team without a weakness.

Time. And the Italians. Or the Argentinians . . . or the West Germans will tell. It is, I suppose, too much to ask that it could be the Scots who find the fault.

There's no harm in wishful thinking!

However, there is certainly nothing in the record book to justify even a slight swagger in the swish of the kilt.

Scotland . . . Five in a Row

We have played Brazil seven times, and have yet to experience the thrill of a win . . . although we did come close in 1974. That was one of two World Cup meetings we have had with the South Americans.

It was in Frankfurt on a warm June night in 1974 that Scotland laid a finger on glory, only to see it slip away. The Scots had just come off a high, having four days earlier recorded their FIRST EVER victory in the Final stages of the World Cup, a 2-0 win over Zaire.

The Scots fans in the 62,000 crowd on Tuesday June 18 were beginning to think the unthinkable: Scotland could qualify if they beat the Brazilians.

The Zaire game was Denis Law's 56th and last Scotland cap. Willie Morgan, younger and fresher, was brought in by manager Willie Ormond for the awesome task against Brazil.

Prime Minister Harold Wilson was there (probably because there were three Leeds players in the Scotland side!).

And after surviving a swirling opening 20 minutes which saw David Harvey save brilliantly from Rivelino, Marinho shudder the cross bar with a volley and Sandy Jardine kicking another effort clear on the line . . . Scotland settled.

And the man the Brazilian journalists called 'the little giant' took over. Scotland captain Billy Bremner, all red-haired fire and Stirling fury, began to take control of mid-field. A situation which didn't please Rivelino who was booked for a nasty foul on the Scottish captain.

Bremner's answer was that familiar pasty-faced smile. And a wee touch of retribution here and there.

The Leeds man could be outplayed: he could never be overawed.

By half-time with the score at 0-0, it was learned that Yugoslavia were leading 6-0 against Zaire on their way to a 9-goal victory.

Brazil add a bit of beef

Careca of **Brazil**, a highly-rated striker by his team-mates and one that the Scotland defence should keep a wary eye on.

Scotland: Five in a Row

Brazil would just need a draw and a 3-0 win in the final game over the Africans to qualify. Scotland knew a win was needed. And set about getting it.

Inspired by Bremner. Urged on by Davie Hay. Fuelled by tremendous support from the travelling 12,000 fans. It was a heady mixture which looked like blowing the Brazilians away.

Their keeper Leao saved well from Hay. A Peter Lorimer special just failed.

And then came the moment the dream died. The goal-keeper Leao parried a shot, knocking the ball straight to the lurking Bremner just a yard or so from goal. But he was caught unprepared, and allowed the ball to bobble off his shinguards and past the post. The moment of destiny was lost. As Burns says in Tam O'Shanter: 'like the snow falls in the river, a moment white then melts forever'.

Scotland's team that June evening was: Harvey; Jardine, McGrain; Holton, Buchan, Bremner; Hay, Dalglish, Jordan, Morgan, Lorimer.

The next time the teams met in the World Cup was eight years later to the day . . . June 18, 1982 before a 47,000 crowd in Seville, Spain.

Again it was a second match into the series. Scotland were off to a 5-2 flier against New Zealand; Brazil had eased past Russia 2-1.

There was a lone piper in the Stadium, heard only fitfully above the samba drums . . . except for the magic moment when big Dave Narey silenced the jungle beat with a raging 25 yard shot into the roof of the net.

'Toe poke' it was called by a well known English TV pundit, whose name esapes me but never escapes the fans.

But the intense heat, which dehydrated many of the Scots players, took its toll. Particularly after Zico equalised for Brazil before half-time with an exquisite free kick from the edge of the box.

Brazil add a bit of beef

Alan Rough knew what to expect. But couldn't do anything about the expected, on a night where he was celebrating his 50th cap.

The leaden-legged Scots sank without trace in the second 45 minutes. Oscar with a close-in header; Eder with a delicate lob and Falcao with a thundering shot all put the ball past Rough.

The Scotland team was: Rough; Narey, F. Gray; Souness, Hansen, Miller; Strachan (sub Dalglish), Hartford (sub McLeish), Archibald, Wark, Robertson.

The full list of games between the countries is:

1966	(Hampden, friendly)	Scotland 1 (Chalmers) Brazil 1
1972	(Rio, friendly)	Brazil 1 Scotland 0
1973	(Hampden, friendly)	Scotland 0 Brazil 1
1974	(Germany W.C.)	Scotland 0 Brazil 0
1977	(Rio, friendly)	Brazil 2 Scotland 0
1982	(Spain, W.C.)	Scotland 1 (Narey) Brazil 4
1987	(Hampden, friendly)	Scotland 0 Brazil 2

There is another reason, of course, why so many of Brazil's top stars are playing outwith the country: finance.

The Brazilian football set-up is deeply in the red and to earn any real money the players move. There is also severe criticism of the organisation of Brazilian football and the amount of violent play in their games.

With so many of their top players out of the country, it is little wonder that the scoring skills and ability of stay-at-home Bebeto have made him the No. 1 attraction.

His real name is José Roberto Gama de Oliveira, which makes the use of nicknames like Bebeto essential, otherwise football match reports would run into thousands of words.

Bebeto, who is now 25, is a slight, almost tiny figure. But he makes up for lack of stature in speed of thought, action and control.

Scotland: Five in a Row

Which is why there was uproar when he made an unexpected, and distinctly unpopular move from the Flamengo club to Vasca last summer. His contract had expired, and the Flamengo club fully expected him to follow the well-trod path to Europe.

But instead he worked a secret deal with their great rivals, which included the player apparently paying £300,000 for his own transfer. The money, of course, had been given to him by Vasco.

The whole deal was clearly the Brazilian equivalent of the Mo Johnston affair in Scotland!

Bebeto's form has been such that national team boss Lazaroni is now trying to find out a way in which he can field his 'dream' forward line of Careca, Romario and Bebeto.

One man's dream can be another man's nightmare . . . if that attack clicks, every other World Cup boss will be waking in the night screaming.

The Brazilian squad is likely to be made up of these players:

Taffarel	Goalkeeper. From the Porto Alegre club in Brazil and reckoned to have put an end to the country's search for a reliable keeper.
Aldair	Defender. With Benfica in Portugal. A big strong player who is likely to be given the job of marking either McCoist or Johnston.
Jorginho	Defender. Likes going forward in attack and an accurate passer. Plays in German football with Leverkusen.
Mozer	Tall, athletic defender who is one of the two candidates for the sweeper role. Very powerful in the air. Plays with Marseilles in France.

Brazil add a bit of beef

Branco Can operate at left back or in midfield. He is starring with Porto in Portuguese football.

Rocha Defender. Another stay-at-home who plays with Sao Paulo. Operates on the left side as a marker, but again very good at initiating attacks and passes well.

Mauro Galvao Based in Rio with the Botafoga club, he is one of the biggest men in the squad and is favourite for the sweeper's job.

Alemao Midfield player based in Italian football with Napoli. Solid tackler and superb passer.

Dunga Another talented midfield man, and another plying his trade in Italian football with Fiorentina.

Valdo The midfield general of the side. He is in Portugal with Benfica. Covers a lot of ground as he moves everywhere to direct operations.

Silas Another who has moved on to Portuguese football. Can operate in midfield or attack. Not big, but nimble and aggressive.

Careca Striker who is rated by his team-mate Diego Maradona as 'the best in the World'. Has played a major part in Napoli's success in Italian football in the past year.

Romario Small, quick striker who has been a tremendous hit in Dutch football with PSV Eindhoven.

Bebeto A small, agile striker who has forced his way into the Brazilian national plans because of his form with his club Vasco and also the international squad while deputising for Careca.

Scotland: Five in a Row

Also likely to feature are defenders Andrez Cruz, Josimar, Mazinho and Ricardo; midfielders Geovani and Tita and striker Muller who is with Torino.

The Stars to Watch . . .

ALL THE WORLD CUP IS A STAGE. But not all the players will be big enough to command it. There are a dozen or so who will undoubtedly battle for the title of star of stars.

And there will be unknowns who will use the event as a springboard to higher things.

But mainly, the public eye will be on the established names. Multi-million pound players who have either done it in the World Cup before, or have hit the headlines for club or country in the past four years. Here are men who will be in the public eye in Italy:

José René Higuita, 22. Long-haired, eccentric and extremely talented goalkeeper with the Columbian team. Loves nothing better than dashing out of his goal to make clearances halfway up the pitch. The only thing he likes better is . . . taking penalties! He has scored nearly 30 for his club Nacional and a few more for his country. Could move into European football in Spain or Italy after the World Cup.

Klaus Augenthaler. This big powerful West German defender is famous not just for stopping opponents, but for the ferocity of his long-range shooting. Rangers found that out when they played against Bayern in last season's European Cup.

At 33, Augenthaler knows this will be his last World Cup and is determined to go one better than the runners-up medal he earned with the German squad in 1986.

Scotland: Five in a Row

Dragan Stojkovic, 25. The undoubted star of the Yugoslavian squad, as Scotland learned to their cost in the second half of the game with the Slavs in Zagreb in the qualifying section. Was spotted as a future internationalist at 18 and won his first cap soon after. Cost Red Star a set of floodlights and five players when they signed Serbia-born Stojkovic from the smaller Radnicki side. Now his midfield talent has been valued at £5 million, the sum Marseilles have agreed to pay to lure him to France next season.

Enzo Francescoli, 28. A wandering Uruguayan who has been with a couple of clubs in his own country before moving to France to play for Racing and ultimately Marseilles. A swift, skilful attacker, as Scotland will remember from the last World Cup. When Uruguay were reduced to 10 men against Scotland in Mexico, they left Francescoli up front on his own. Which was more than enough for the Scots defence, who found him hard to hold. A former South American Footballer of the Year, he cost Marseilles £2 million.

Careca. Or to give the brightest of Brazilian stars his full name, Antonio de Oliveira Filho. It's understandable that the Latins like to give themselves short, snappy playing names! Has been a star in Brazil since the age of 17, then three years ago moved to Italy to play alongside Maradona for Napoli, a partnership of awesome talent. Missed the 1982 World Cup because of injury, but was outstanding for his country four years later in Mexico. Cost Napoli £3 million, but has been a prolific scorer in a League where goals are gained the hard way. Now 29.

Diego Armando Maradona. Now 29, troubled by injury, weighed down by success but certainly not strapped for cash! The World's No. 1 player for the past decade, he captained Argentina to their World Cup victory in Mexico

Diego Maradona, entertainer supreme.

in 1986 and had a hand in putting England out of the competition en route! He moved to European football for massive sums, yet never quite hit it off with his first club Barcelona because of injury and illness, and was transferred to Napoli for a staggering £5 millon. Initially was a tremendous success in Italian football, but in the past year or so has had several skirmishes with the club and could be on the move again later this year.

Scotland: Five in a Row

Marco van Basten. One of the most exciting strikers in Europe, who was voted European Footballer of the Year in 1988 . . . the year after his club and country colleague Ruud Gullit had won the same award. Tall and elegant, the 25-year-old from Utrecht joined Ajax as a teenager and in successive seasons scored enough goals to be top marksman in his country four times in a row. That was enough to persuade A.C. Milan to fork out £1.5 million (a paltry sum compared to what they would have to pay now) to take him to Italy in 1987. Reputed to be the highest-paid footballer in Europe, he is certainly a millionaire, and if, as expected, Holland have a good World Cup, his value would be mind-blowing.

Bebeto (or José Roberto Gama de Oliveira if you prefer). 26-year-old who has become a star at home in Brazil, but is expected to follow the European trail like so many others of his countrymen. Small, slight, but quick and brave, he can operate in midfield or up front. Has been nicknamed 'the new Zico' and is the current South American Footballer of the Year. Featured in a dramatic £300,000 transfer from Flamengo to Vasco da Gama (with a bit of crafty dealing by his new club who paid the money into Bebeto's own bank account to let him buy his own transfer).

Romario. This 24-year-old striker was an outstanding success in the 1988 Olympics, and immediately cashed in on his reputation for multi-bucks to join PSV Eindhoven in Dutch football in a £3 million move from Vasco da Gama. A player with the instinctive poacher's sense for goals anywhere in the box. Has quickly become leading scorer in both Dutch domestic and European scoring charts.

Jurgen Klinsman, 25. West German star who joined the trek to Italian football a year ago to join Inter-Milan where he has been banging in the goals. Was top scorer in the German League in 1988 which won him his place in the national side

The Stars to Watch . . .

The elegant Marco Van Basten of Holland.

where he forms a lethal partnership with the more experienced Rudi Voller, who is also playing in Italian football, with Roma.

Alexander Zavarov, 29. Russian midfield star who is now earning a professional career in Italian football with Juventus. Former Soviet Player of the Year, he moved from Kiev to Juventus three seasons ago for £3 million. Took a while to settle in Italy, but is expected to be a star for the formidable Russian side. Which makes a change from a few years back where he was suspended for life (later reprieved) for too much drinking!

Gianluca Vialla. This 25-year-old former winger is now regarded as Italy's main striker. His club Sampdoria are said to value him at more than £7 million. Has played almost 50 times for Italy since he made his debut as sub against Poland in 1985. Is said to be the best Italian striker since the legendary Paolo Rossi, but has still to fulfill that potential. Mainly because the Italians are still searching for the right striking partner. They hope to have that sorted out before the battle begins in earnest in Rome on June 9 against Austria.

Gary Lineker, 28. Came back to British football last summer after two years in Spanish football with Barcelona. Lineker, from Leicester, started his career with his home-town club as an apprentice and within a few years became the club's top scorer for four successive seasons. This brought him an £800,000 move to Everton in 1985. He had already been capped by England . . . his first honour coming against Scotland at Hampden in 1984 when he came on as substitute . . . at Leicester. But it was after his move to Merseyside that it all began to happen for snooker fanatic Lineker. In the 1986 World Cup Finals in Mexico a hat-trick against Poland helped him on his way to six goals and the

The Stars to Watch . . .

Gianluca Vialla of Italy.

Scotland: Five in a Row

Gary Lineker, striking for England.

honour of being top marksman in the competition. Which in turn brought an offer from Barcelona which Everton could not refuse . . . £2.75 million. When the time came to quit Spain, Lineker was offered a lucrative deal in Monaco, but elected to return to England and Spurs. His pace and strength make him a key figure in the England set-up alongside Peter Beardsley of Liverpool.

The Games, the Guys and the Goals

Oslo, September 14, 1988

Norway 1   Scotland 2

Scorers: Norway — Fjortoft (43 mins).
Scotland — McStay (14) Johnston (62).

Team: Leighton; Gillespie, McLeish, Miller, Malpas; Aitken (sub. Durrant), McStay, Nicol; Gallacher, McClair, Johnston.
Subs not used: Goram, MacLeod, Narey, Sharp.
Attendance: 22,769.

Hampden, October 19, 1988

Scotland 1   Yugoslavia 1

Scorers: Scotland — Johnston (16 mins).
Yugoslavia — Katanec (36).

Team: Goram; Gough, McLeish, Miller, Malpas; Nicol, McStay, Aitken (sub Speedie), Bett (sub McCoist); McClair, Johnston.
Subs not used: Gunn, MacLeod, Gallacher.
Attendance: 42,771.

Cyprus, February 8, 1989

Cyprus 2   Scotland 3

Scotland: Five in a Row

Scorers: Cyprus — Koliandris (14 mins) Ioannou (47)
Scotland — Johnston (8), Gough (53, 89)

Team: Leighton; Gough, Narey, McLeish, Malpas;
Nicol (sub. Ian Ferguson), Aitken, McStay,
Speedie (sub McInally); McClair, Johnston.
Subs not used: Goram, Nicholas, Gallacher.
Attendance: 20,000.

Hampden, March 8, 1989

Scotland 2   France 0

Scorer: Johnston (28 mins, 52).

Team: Leighton; Gough, McLeish, Gillespie, Malpas;
Nicol, Ferguson (sub Strachan), McStay, Aitken;
McCoist (sub McClair), Johnston.
Subs not used: Goram, Speedie, Gallacher.
Attendance: 65,204.

Hampden, April 26, 1989

Scotland 2   Cyprus 1

Scorers: Scotland — Johnston (26 mins) McCoist (65).
Cyprus — Nicolaou (63).

Team: Leighton; McLeish, McPherson, Malpas; Gough,
McStay, Aitken, Durie (sub Speedie); Nevin (sub
Nicholas), McCoist, Johnston.
Subs not used: Goram, Jim McInally, Gallacher.
Attendance: 50,081.

Zagreb, September 6, 1989

Yugoslavia 3   Scotland 1

Scorers: Yugoslavia — Katanec (54 mins), Nicol (57 o.g.),
Gillespie (58 o.g.).
Scotland — Durie (37).

The Games, the Guys and the Goals

Team: Leighton; Gillespie, McLeish, Miller, Malpas; Nicol, Aitken, McStay, MacLeod, McCoist, Durie (sub Alan McInally).
Subs not used: Goram, Clarke, Grant, McClair.
Attendance: 40,000.

Paris, October 11, 1989

France 3   Scotland 0

Scorers: Deschamps (20 mins), Cantona (62), Durand (88).

Team: Leighton; Nicol, Gough, McLeish, Malpas; Strachan (sub A. McInally), Aitken, McStay, MacLeod (sub Bett); McCoist, Johnston.
Subs not used: Goram, Miller, McClair.
Attendance: 25,000.

Hampden, November 15, 1989

Scotland 1   Norway 1

Scorers: Scotland — McCoist (44 mins).
Norway — Johnsen (89).

Team: Leighton; McPherson, McLeish, Miller (sub McLeod), Malpas; Aitken, McStay, Bett; McCoist, Johnston, Cooper (sub McClair).
Subs not used: Goram, Clarke, Nevin.
Attendance: 63,987.

Scotland's World Cup Record

SWITZERLAND 1954

SCOTLAND	0	AUSTRIA	1
SCOTLAND	0	URUGUAY	7

SWEDEN 1958

(Qualifying)

SCOTLAND	4	SPAIN	2
SPAIN	4	SCOTLAND	1
SWITZERLAND	1	SCOTLAND	2
SCOTLAND	3	SWITZERLAND	2

(Final Stages)

SCOTLAND	1	YUGOSLAVIA	1
SCOTLAND	2	PARAGUAY	3
SCOTLAND	1	FRANCE	2

CHILE 1962

(Qualifying)

SCOTLAND	4	REP. OF IRELAND	1
REP. OF IRELAND	0	SCOTLAND	3
CZECHOSLOVAKIA	4	SCOTLAND	0
SCOTLAND	3	CZECHOSLOVAKIA	2

PLAY-OFF MATCH IN BRUSSELS

CZECHOSLOVAKIA	4	SCOTLAND	2

(After extra-time) (Did not qualify)

Scotland's World Cup Record

ENGLAND 1966

(Qualifying)

SCOTLAND	3	FINLAND	1
POLAND	1	SCOTLAND	1
FINLAND	1	SCOTLAND	2
SCOTLAND	1	POLAND	2
SCOTLAND	1	ITALY	0
ITALY	3	SCOTLAND	0

(Did not qualify)

MEXICO 1970

(Qualifying)

SCOTLAND	2	AUSTRIA	1
CYPRUS	0	SCOTLAND	5
SCOTLAND	1	WEST GERMANY	1
SCOTLAND	8	CYPRUS	0
AUSTRIA	2	SCOTLAND	0
WEST GERMANY	3	SCOTLAND	2

(Did not qualify)

WEST GERMANY 1974

(Qualifying)

DENMARK	1	SCOTLAND	4
SCOTLAND	2	DENMARK	0
SCOTLAND	2	CZECHOSLOVAKIA	1
CZECHOSLOVAKIA	1	SCOTLAND	0

(Final Stages)

SCOTLAND	2	ZAIRE	0
SCOTLAND	0	BRAZIL	0
SCOTLAND	1	YUGOSLAVIA	1

Scotland: Five in a Row

ARGENTINA 1978

(Qualifying)

CZECHOSLOVAKIA	2	SCOTLAND	0
SCOTLAND	1	WALES	0
SCOTLAND	3	CZECHOSLOVAKIA	1
WALES	0	SCOTLAND	2

(Final Stages)

SCOTLAND	1	PERU	3
SCOTLAND	1	IRAN	1
SCOTLAND	3	HOLLAND	2

SPAIN 1982

(Qualifying)

SWEDEN	0	SCOTLAND	1
SCOTLAND	0	PORTUGAL	0
ISRAEL	0	SCOTLAND	1
SCOTLAND	1	NORTHERN IRELAND	1
SCOTLAND	3	ISRAEL	1
SCOTLAND	2	SWEDEN	0
NORTHERN IRELAND	0	SCOTLAND	0
PORTUGAL	2	SCOTLAND	1

(Final Stages)

SCOTLAND	5	NEW ZEALAND	2
SCOTLAND	1	BRAZIL	4
SCOTLAND	2	USSR	2

MEXICO 1986

(Qualifying)

SCOTLAND	3	ICELAND	0
SCOTLAND	3	SPAIN	1
SPAIN	1	SCOTLAND	0
SCOTLAND	0	WALES	1
ICELAND	0	SCOTLAND	1
WALES	1	SCOTLAND	1

PLAY-OFF MATCHES

SCOTLAND	2	AUSTRALIA	0
AUSTRALIA	0	SCOTLAND	0

(Final Stages)

SCOTLAND	0	DENMARK	1
SCOTLAND	1	WEST GERMANY	2
SCOTLAND	0	URUGUAY	0

Parliamo Italscozie

'**A**NDIAMO, ANDY E MO.' This could be the rallying cry for the tartan lads in Italy this summer. Roughly translated, it means 'let's go, Andy and Mo.' Almost World Cup song material in fact.

The Scots will be assured of a warm welcome from the locals . . . as long as they behave. Lads, if there are any kilt-lifters among you, restrain yourselves. All you do is prove that we are indeed a small nation!

Throughout the World Cup campaign, while England's tearaways have been wrecking Stockholm and the like, the Scots have trekked from Norway, to Cyprus, to Yugoslavia and to Paris with scarcely an ill comment.

I sometimes wonder if it is just the thrawn bit in the Scots that has worked this welcome trick. The more the English misbehave, the better we will become seems to be the motto. It's a good one.

Some words of advice . . . and some words that might be useful.

DON'T run up a bar bill. Pay as you go means less pain as you go.

BEWARE in restaurants if you think the steaks and the sole are cheap. Check the prices are not based on l'etto, which is 100 grammes. That's just four ounces. So a steak weighing in at 1lb will be four times the menu price. I don't know what the Italian is for 'does you does, or does you don't take Access': but it might be worth learning.

I do know a little Parliamo Italiano, some of which might come in useful.

Scotland: Five in a Row

Andiamo . . . . as you know, is let's go. Can double up for here we go.

Basta . . . . is not what you think. Don't start taking umbrage. It just means enough: to be used if you think the measures are too big.

Che cosa . . . . what is.

Che sono questi . . . . what are these (pointing to the strange ojects on your plate).

Due bicchieri . . . . two glasses (of whatever amber fluid has taken your fancy).

Che cosa prende? . . . . what will you have? (useful for making friends with the locals).

Come sta? . . . . how are you?

Grazie . . . . thanks.

Ho sete . . . . I am thirsty.

Abbiamo fame . . . . we are hungry.

La piu grande del mondo . . . the biggest in the world (a phrase to be used with discretion).

Entrata . . . . entrance.

Uscita . . . . exit.

E la tua amica? . . . . is this your friend? (useful at chatting up time).

Cotta bene . . . . well cooked (just how you like your steak).

Piu grande . . . . bigger (just how you like your steak!)
Per piacere . . . . please.

Pieno . . . . full (as in as a wilk).

Sotto la tavola . . . . under the table (see above).

Non ho denaro . . . . I have no money (may be handy at the end of two weeks).

Parliamo Italscozie

Il pisello . . . . pea (the vegetable, of course).

Quanti . . . . what a lot of (fill in your own word depending on the game).

La mancia . . . . tip (if you have anything left).

Peccato! . . . . too bad (useful if you meet any Costa Rican fans).

Il sogno . . . . dream (as in Scotland 3 Sweden 0).

Mi fai un favore, Jimmy . . . . do us a favour, Jimmy.

Finally, one for any of the ladies who are dragged along on the pretence that it is a holiday:

Mi fa male la testa . . . . I have a headache.

Scotland: Five in a Row

WORLD CUP SCORE-SHEET

Group A

Italy .... v Austria ....
USA .... v Czechoslovakia ...
Italy .... v USA ....
Austria .... v Czechoslovakia ...
Italy .... v Czechoslovakia ...
Austria .... v USA ....

Group B

Argentina ..... v Cameroon ....
USSR .... v Romania ......
Argentina ..... v USSR ....
Cameroon .... v Romania ......
Argentina ..... v Romania ......
Cameroon .... v USSR ....

Group C

Brazil .... v Sweden ....
Costa Rica .... v Scotland ......
Brazil .... v Costa Rica ...
Sweden .... v Scotland ......
Brazil .... v Scotland ......
Sweden .... v Costa Rica ...

Group D

UAE .... v Colombia ....
W Germany .. v Yugoslavia ....
Yugoslavia ... v Colombia ....
W Germany .. v UAE ....
Yugoslavia ... v UAE ....
W Germany .. v Colombia ....

Group E

Belgium .... v S Korea ....
Uruguay ...... v Spain ....
Belgium .... v Uruguay ......
S Korea .... v Spain ....
Belgium .... v Spain ....
S Korea .... v Uruguay ......

Group F

England .... v Rep of Ire .....
Holland .... v Egypt ....
England .... v Holland ....
Rep of Ire ..... v Egypt ....
England .... v Egypt ....
Rep of Ire ..... v Holland ....

SECOND ROUND

June 23

.... v .... (Naples)
.... v .... (Bari)

June 24

.... v .... (Turin)
.... v .... (Milan)

June 25

.... v .... (Rome)
.... v .... (Genoa)

June 26

.... v .... (Bologna)
.... v .... (Verona)

QUARTER FINALS

June 30

.... v .... (Rome)
.... v .... (Florence)

July 1

.... v .... (Naples)
.... v .... (Milan)

SEMI FINALS

July 3

.... v .... (Naples)

July 4

.... v .... (Turin)

THIRD-PLACE PLAY-OFF

July 7

.... v .... (Bari)

FINAL
(Rome, July 8, 7pm)

.... v ....